William Penn: The Life and Legacy o
Pennsyl\

By Charles Riv\

About Charles River Editors

Charles River Editors provides superior editing and original writing services across the digital publishing industry, with the expertise to create digital content for publishers across a vast range of subject matter. In addition to providing original digital content for third party publishers, we also republish civilization's greatest literary works, bringing them to new generations of readers via ebooks.

Sign up here to receive updates about free books as we publish them, and visit Our Kindle Author Page to browse today's free promotions and our most recently published Kindle titles.

Introduction

Frederick S. Lamb's painting of a young William Penn

William Penn

Of all the original 13 colonies in America, only one owes its conception to one man, and indeed, Pennsylvania was and still remains bound up in the life and character of its founder, William Penn. Here was a man born into a military family who saw his father rise through the ranks of the 17th century English court to become a friend of the king, and he even considered a military career for himself, only to leave it all behind to become a member of the "Society of Friends," known colloquially as the Quakers.

Few today know much about the Quakers. Whenever the subject of Quakerism slips into conversation, most picture a rosy-cheeked fellow in a simple black overcoat, and a wide brim hat atop his thick, cloud-white hair, inspired by the famous logo of the Quaker Oats company. In spite of the stereotype, Quakers today come in all colors, shapes, and sizes, with the more liberal folk sporting trendy haircuts, tattoos, and various piercings. They call themselves "Friends," a starkly different but very devout following of God. They strive for a world empowered by peace and acceptance, an ambitious mission fueled by diversity, blind to race, gender, or creed.

As amicably harmless as the Friends might appear, there was once a time when being a Quaker was at the very best an instant conviction, and at the very worst a death sentence. Their unorthodox ideals were considered poisonous and potentially dangerous by authorities, who would fight time and time again to stamp out the flames of their movement, but still, they weathered storm after storm. And while the peace-loving followers of Christ were famed for their views of harmony, by no means were they feeble opponents. Not only would they persevere in the face of persecution, theirs was a movement so powerful that it stood strong for centuries, and much of that was due to William Penn's work in North America.

For all his love of the sect and its plain ways, he was himself quite a scholar, able to debate some of the greatest minds of his age and win. He was also an ambitious man who saw the answer to his people's persecution not in capitulation but in building a new society where all people could be free to worship God in the way each felt right. Along the way he befriended kings and scoundrels and suffered at the hands of each, only to triumph repeatedly, until finally he experienced what was, for the people of his faith, the ultimate triumph of death, knowing that the colony he had founded was thriving and would likely do so for generations to come.

William Penn: The Life and Legacy of the English Quaker Who Founded Pennsylvania chronicles the life of one of colonial America's most important figures. Along with pictures of important people, places, and events, you will learn about William Penn like never before.

The Quakers

The prelude to the Quakers' story goes all the way back to the mid-17th century – more precisely, the English Civil War. Unlike most wars, the seed of the war had not been planted by revolutionaries who sought to usurp the throne with their own brand of government. Rather, the discontented public had become piqued by the overbearing religious authority. It would not be long before the brewing tension escalated into violent conflict.

Critics of the monarch were often pointed to the so-called "Divine Right of Kings," which granted monarchs (at the time Charles I) the right to rule by will of God. These kings were supposedly endorsed by God Himself, which might have made sense to the royals but was head-scratching logic for the public. The restless people called for a more equal balance in power between the King and Parliament, which they believed was their only chance of getting their voices heard.

Most of all, religious tensions stemming from longstanding and ongoing conflicts between the Protestants and Roman Catholics had riled up the public. In 1625, the year King Charles I rose to the throne, he married a sharp-nosed and raven-haired Catholic beauty, Henrietta Maria of France. Included in their marriage treaty was a stipulation that allowed Henrietta to practice her faith without persecution. It also ensured that her fellow Catholics could excuse themselves from Anglican services without penalty.

Charles I of England

Henrietta Maria of France

This startled the largely Protestant public, awakening a fear that hit far too close to home. The horrific reign of Queen Mary I was only less than a century ago, and the carnage that resulted in the queen's determination to revert England to Catholicism was still fresh in their minds. In an attempt to wipe out Protestantism in England, the queen burned at least 300 Protestant "heretics" at the stake, becoming the muse to the nickname and urban legend of "Bloody Mary."

Tensions with nonconformists reached an all-time high when their freedom of speech was stripped from them. In 1637, a trio of prolific Puritan pamphleteers, William Prynne, Henry Burton, and John Bastwick, were charged with "seditious libel." Their ears were sliced off, and the letters "S.L." were marked onto their cheeks with a blistering-hot branding iron as a reminder of their crimes.

Outright war was close at hand. That same year, when King Charles I attempted to revise the prayer book, the first wave of riots erupted in Edinburgh. The revisions, which many believed reeked of Catholic motives, enraged Scottish Presbyterians, who were now on a mission to take back their freedom of worship. In response, the king simply curbed the riots, the public protests falling on his deaf ears. The king hustled to push the sanctioned prayer book, and made examples of those who refused.

On August 22, 1642, civil war was officially declared, one that would rage on for 9 years straight. With the help of the Puritan Oliver Cromwell, Parliament would win the war, but when Cromwell died in 1658, Charles' son, Charles II, would make his way to the throne, 3 years later.

Cromwell

Charles II of England

Meanwhile, the Anglican bishops Charles II had appointed took the driver's seat on national matters, once again hoping to bring back the religious uniformity that Laud had once fought for. In 1662, the Act of Uniformity was issued, which called for all the churches in England to abide by the same set of prayers, ceremonies, and sacrament administration according to The Book of Common Prayer. All ministers, pastors, and religious leaders, regardless of sect, were made to sign an oath that prohibited them from straying from the good book and "endeavor[ing] any change or alteration of government, either in church or state."

As these events were playing out, in July of 1624, in a small Puritan village known as Drayton-in-the-Clay, just a few miles from Leicester, baby George was welcomed into the Fox household. George was the oldest of 4 children in a middle class family, born to Christopher Fox, a weaver by trade, and his wife, Mary Lago.

A plaque commemorating Fox's birthplace

A portrait believed to depict Fox

Unlike the dark pasts shared by some of history's most influential figures, George, raised in a Puritan household, had a relatively comfortable childhood. That said, some uncertainty still exists as to what George Fox was truly like. Like many boys his age, George learned to read and write, but little is known about his formal education. What was widely known was his intrigue with God and religion at an early age, as well as his observant disposition, which seemed to be beyond his years. At the age of 11, he exhibited an obsession in living a life of "pureness and righteousness." While other children busied themselves with games and socializing with their friends, George was said to have been deconstructing the Lord's word and applying it to his daily interactions. The self-aware George described his experience in his autobiography, writing, "I had a gravity and stayedness of mind and spirit, not usual in children."

All it took was one event to rock 19-year-old George's world. In the summer of 1643, George visited a local fair with one of his cousins, where the pair met up with some mutual friends. When the festivities began to wind down, the group decided to stop at a nearby bar for a quick pint. George had never been much of a drinker, but not wanting to dampen the mood, he took them up on their offer, and ordered a glass for himself. Within seconds, the rowdy group had knocked back their first glasses and were thumping the counters with their fists, hollering for another round. They had planned on returning to the festival, but the tipsy men were now challenging each other to a drinking game. Whoever refused to drink, they announced, would be responsible for all their tabs at the end of the night.

George's hot ears rang with disbelief. How dare these men be so bold as to suggest such a thing? Not even his non-Christian acquaintances had ever ventured such a hedonistic act. The man of few words, as always, had little to say. He simply paid for his drink and exited the pub, feeling lost and dejected. That night, George paced round and round in his room, his insomnia triggered by the spiritual labyrinth he had inadvertently stumbled into. He negotiated for hours with God through prayer and silent reflection, begging for answers to the questions flooding his mind. In the midst of his prayer fest, an internal voice that he believed came from God spoke to him. The voice proclaimed, "You see how young people go together into frivolity, and old people into the earth; you must leave all, young and old, keep out of all, and be as a stranger to all."

A part of George was hesitant about leaving behind a family he so dearly loved, but God's message was loud and clear, and it was one that could not be ignored. A few months later, George packed up his essentials and left the cozy town. For years, he roamed, flitting from one religious sect to the next, in pursuit of the truth behind the word of God. George's deep depression was laden over a simmering existential crisis, which made for a tough journey, and was made even more difficult with the volatile background of the civil war. First, he found himself in Barnet, a market town by London. As a young male, George, only human, felt the enticements of the temptations that lay in the neighboring resort town. To repel these temptations, he either shuttered himself in his room or took extensive walks in the calming countryside, finding a friend in nature.

Over the next 4 years, George continued his search for a solution to his spiritual distress, vigorously hounding an assortment of clergymen from various sects and backgrounds. During the turbulent ride, he kept his Bible close at hand, scanning page after page of Scripture for enlightenment. He encountered a wide range of religious experts who aimed to help him overcome his spiritual unease, only to be met with one failure after another. For example, one minister from Warwickshire advised him to incorporate tobacco and psalm-singing into a ritualistic ceremony, but George did not care for it. Another clergyman suggested bloodletting, the antiquated process of extracting blood as a means to alleviate physical and psychological ailments. Legend had it that not a blood of drop could be extracted from George, as he was completely drained from the spiritual emptiness inside of him.

From that point on, the obstacles of George's spiritual quest seemed to evaporate, and he began to chance upon the very answers he had been searching for the entire time. Though he was still physically present on Earth, George claimed that he had now elevated himself to a higher dimension, one that had seen the Kingdom of God. Only 2 paths existed that would bring one to the Heavenly Kingdom – one that was rampant with death and despair, and the other with pure love and light, which would ultimately lead them to God's side. An excerpt from George's journal reads, "I was taken up in the love of God...it was opened to me by the eternal light and power...and I...clearly saw that all was done and to be done in and by Christ, and how He conquers and destroys this tempter, the devil, and all his works..."

These "openings," as George called them, provided the process of understanding what it took to walk on the path of purity, its instructions divulged to him in a chain of fully-realized revelations. Based on George's divine disclosures, Jesus Christ was the Holy Light that inspirited and enlightened all of mankind, and the secret to understanding Him could be unlocked within oneself. If one were to listen closely and serve the Lord without grievances, they, too, could be transformed by the Light, and made pure in the name of Christ.

In addition to these openings, George was said to have been blessed with divine, magical powers, including the resurrection of the dead. His enlightenment also gifted him with psychic-like abilities, and he had allegedly predicted a number of English disasters and war victors with chilling accuracy, such as the Great Fire of London. He even foretold the assassinations of many famous folk, including his own, thereby dodging his own would-be deaths on multiple instances.

George had heard his calling – it had become his mission to spread the word about his new revelations. Many found the Quaker ideals fresh and exhilarating, but authorities were appalled by these "toxic" practices. The vision on Pendle Hill had unfettered George of any iota of doubt that remained in his system. In less than 3 years, Quaker venues hosted by George and his followers attracted over a thousand attendees each time. It was at this point that authorities began to seriously regard the Quakers as a serious threat. Some accused them of witchcraft, and others of conspiring to overthrow the government. Authorities decided to nip the problem in the bud before it spread, and in 1655, George was arrested in Whetstone Village and sent to London. In London, George was taken to Cromwell, and the Lord Protector of the Commonwealth of England. After an unusually calm and civil conversation, George assured Cromwell that the Quakers had no interest in the government. By the end of their talk, Cromwell, too, was allegedly so moved by his words that his eyes welled up with tears at the time of George's departure. Cromwell vowed to welcome his new friend into his home at any time.

Penn's Early Years

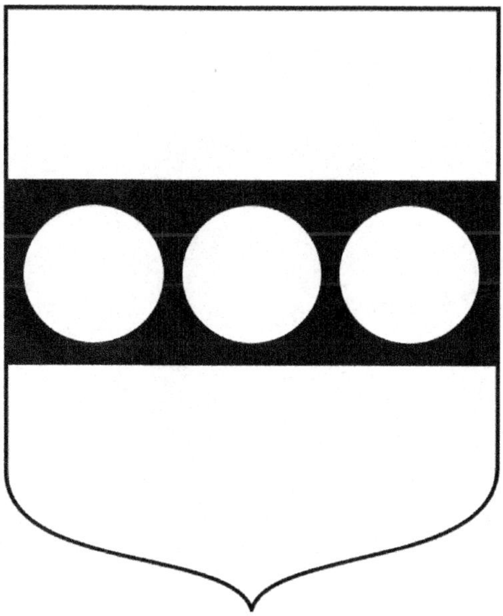

Penn's coat of arms

Almost 20 years after the birth of George Fox, another Quaker legend was born. On October 14, 1644, William Penn was born at Tower Hill in London, just northwest of the Tower of London. Ironically, he grew up in the very real shadow of religious intolerance.

William's father was Sir William Penn, an Admiral in the English Navy. Of his father, the younger Penn later wrote, "William Penn was born at Bristol in 1621, of the ancient family of the Penns of Penn Lodge, Wilts. He was Captain at the age of twenty-one; Rear-Admiral of Ireland at twenty-three; Vice-Admiral of England and General in the first Dutch war, at thirty two. He was subsequently M.P. for Weymouth, Governor of Kingsale, and Vice- Admiral of Munster. He was a highly successful commander, and in 1654 he obtained possession of Jamaica. He was appointed a Commissioner of the Navy in 1660, in which year he was knighted. After the Dutch fight in 1665, where he distinguished himself as second in command under the Duke of York, he took leave of the sea, but continued to act as a Commissioner for the Navy till 1669, when he retired to Wanstead, on account of his bodily infirmities, and dying there, September 16th, 1670, aged forty-nine…"

Sir William Penn

Penn's mother, Margaret Jasper, had been married previously to a Dutch sea captain who left her a young and attractive widow. When her first child was born, her 23-year-old husband was busily working his way up through the ranks fighting Irish Catholics by setting up blockades along the Irish Coast. By the time little William was five years old, Cromwell had won the English Civil War and Charles I had been beheaded, but by the time Penn was an adult, Cromwell was dead and another king sat upon the English throne. Needless to say, all of this ensured Penn learned at an early age the true danger of religious intolerance.

Penn's childhood was far from uneventful on a personal level, too. He survived a bout with the often deadly smallpox but lost his hair, causing him to wear a wig in public until he was an adult. Some three decades later, George Fox wrote to a friend of this situation, "W. Penn when but 3 years old so lost his hair by the small Pox that he wore them then, long & about 6 years before his Convincement, he wore one, & after that he endeavored to go in his own hair…. he wears them to keep his head & ears warm & not for pride; which is manifest in that…his Border, but a five shillings…"

His parents, wanting to shield their son from the taunts of other children about his appearance, moved from London to a country estate in Essex. There the younger Penn developed a lifelong interest in plants and gardening. He also met and spent time with the famed diarist Samuel Pepys, who lived next door.

Pepys

When he became old enough to attend school, Penn's father enrolled him at the local Chigwell School, founded in 1629 by the Archbishop of York. Like most other English schools, it was run by the Anglican Church. There Penn received a classical education and made a name for himself as a runner. While at Chigwell, Penn took on a more serious, even dour demeanor that would last for the rest of his life, and he became interested in spiritual matters. "While…alone in his chamber, being then eleven years old, he was suddenly surprised with an inward comfort and as he thought an external glory in the room, which gave rise to religious emotions, during which he had the strongest conviction of the being of a God, and that the soul of man was capable of enjoying communication with him. He believed also that the seal of Divinity had been put upon him at this moment, or that he had been awakened or called upon to a holy life."

Penn remained in the school several more years until a military defeat disgraced his father and forced the family to move to Ireland, where he was taught by tutors. While in Ireland, at around the age of 15, Penn met Quaker missionary Thomas Loe, who led him to a spiritual encounter during which, he later said, "the Lord visited me and gave me divine Impressions of Himself."

Never one to be kept down for long by either circumstances or loyalty, Admiral Penn returned to England, having offered to help restore the monarchy. His plan succeeded after Charles Stuart was crowned Charles II - the king rewarded him with a knighthood and made him Commissioner of the Navy. This allowed the elder Penn to send his son to Oxford University in 1660, where he trusted the young man would join the ranks of the powerful Cavaliers who ruled the college socially. But young Penn, disturbed by the way in which his own social class mistreated the others in their midst, and feeling a growing connection with the gentle Quakers, decided to avoid all social connections and become something of an intellectual hermit.

Penn was able to maintain his sort of social aloofness while he was at Oxford, but his return home to his parents' life in Charles II's opulent court made him uncomfortable. Eventually, he turned more and more to the world of the mind and the spirit, becoming a disciple of the former Oxford Dean John Owen. Owen had a profound impact on Penn's life, forcing him to evaluate and think carefully about his personal and intellectual beliefs. Penn remained loyal to Owen even when the university fined those students seen in his presence, so his father removed him from school, insisting that, when he was allowed to return, young Penn would follow the rules. Though Penn did return to Oxford, he did not stay long and was soon expelled for refusing to abide by the university's strict religious practices, ones he did not agree with.

Owen

New Directions

William Penn as a young adult

Hoping that some time out of the country and away from court would improve both Penn's behavior and his parent's social standing, Admiral Penn sent his son to Paris, then considered to be Europe's center of art and culture. Not surprisingly, the young man was unimpressed by the fancy manners of the French court and instead turned for company to Moise Amyraut, a Protestant theologian who himself had been ostracized by the Catholic court. Amyraut's philosophy placed significant emphasis on each man's free will to accept or reject God's call on his life. This was antithetical to both Anglican and Puritan teachings, but it appealed to Penn, driving him further down his own individual spiritual search.

Amyraut

Penn returned home in the summer of 1664 and, as is the way of young men when they have learned something new, was anxious to share his experiences with his family and friends. For his part, Pepys was not impressed, confiding to his diary that "after dinner comes Mr. Pen to visit me, and staid an houre talking with me. I perceive something of learning he hath got, but a great deale, if not too much, of the vanity of the French garbe and affected manner of speech and gait. I fear all real profit he hath made of his travel will signify little." This affection for good clothing would plague Penn for much of his life as a Quaker, since his fellows shunned showy garb.

With his son no longer welcome at Oxford, Admiral Penn decided to have the young man study law. This was agreeable to Penn, but his pursuit of a law career was interrupted in 1665 when war with Holland broke out and he decided to try his hand at sea, serving as a go-between for his father and the king. This drew father and son together and led Penn to write, "Honored Father...I pray God, after all the foul weather and dangers you are exposed to, and shall be, that you come home as secure. And I bless God my heart does not in any way fail, but firmly believe that if God has called you out to battle, He will cover your head in that smoky day. And, as I never knew what a father was till I had wisdom enough to prize him, so I can safely say that now, of all times, your concerns are most dear to me."

Admiral Penn did indeed survive the war, but he and his son returned to London as people were dying in massive numbers due to one of the dreaded plagues that were the scourge of Europe during this time. His experiences during the plague proved influential on him, but it did not bring about a conversion. Penn later wrote, "[I]n the time of the great plague in London…the deep sense [God] gave me of the vanity of this world and of the irreligiousness of the religions of it; then of my mournful and bitter cries to Him, that He would show me his own way of life and salvation, and my resolution to follow Him whatever reproaches or suffering it might cost me, and that with great reverence and brokenness of spirit. …after all this, the glory of the world overtook me, and I was even ready to give myself up unto it, seeing as yet no such things as the primitive spirit and church on earth; and being ready to faint concerning my hope of the restitution of all things."

Not quite ready to leave behind the teachings of his youth, Penn returned to Ireland on his father's behalf and served in the British Army against some rebellious Irish peasants. So thrilling did the future pacifist find battle that he seriously considered becoming a career soldier, but if this surprised his friends, they were even more shocked to learn that Admiral Penn had discouraged him, writing in July 1666, "Besides my former advice I can say nothing but advise to sobriety and all those things that will speak you a Christian and a gentleman, which prudence may make to have the best consistency. …I wish your youthful desires mayn't outrun your discretion. … God bless, direct and protect you."

While Penn was in Ireland trying his hand at soldiering, the Great Fire of 1666 broke out and destroyed much of London. Returning home again after the natural disaster, Penn fell into a dark depression. To make matters worse, he also confronted increased religious persecution in his native land. Seeing the Quakers, a group that seemed to want to trouble no one, take the brunt of this mistreatment offended his sense of justice and ultimately pushed him into their arms.

Conscious of how his decisions would impact his family, Penn began quietly, by discreetly attending Quaker meetings in Cork. However if he hoped that the king's power would not reach into distant Ireland, he was wrong. Ultimately, he was arrested, along with Loe and a number of other Quakers, for worshiping illegally.

Knowing that he was the son of a powerful man, and that he had not yet officially joined the sect, the men who arrested him offered him his freedom. Penn rejected this offer and instead publicly joined his friends in the faith and their fate. He did not stop there, however; he also drew upon his legal training to defend himself and the others, reminding the Earl of Orrery that, unlike other religious sects such as the Puritans, the Quakers eschewed political involvement.

“[T]hough to dissent from a national system imposed by authority, renders men heretics; yet I dare believe your lordship is better read in reason and theology, than to subscribe a maxim so vulgar and untrue; for imagining most visible constitutions of religious government suited to the nature and genius of a civil empire, it cannot be esteemed heresy, but to scare a multitude from such inquiries as may create divisions, fatal to a civil policy, and therefore at worst, deserves only the name of Disturbers.”

Penn then took his arguments a step further, drawing on his personal knowledge of the Earl’s status and practice: "But I presume, my Lord, the acquaintance you have had with other countries, must needs have furnished you with this infallible observation: that diversities of faith and worship contribute not to the disturbance of any place, where moral uniformity is barely requisite to preserve the peace. It is not long since you were a good solicitor for the liberty I now crave, and concluded no way so effectual to improve or advantage this country, as to dispense with freedom in things relating to conscience....”

While his judges did not necessarily respect Penn’s arguments, they did respect his father’s position and thus turned him loose to answer directly to Admiral Penn himself. One can only imagine the heated arguments that passed between the two passionate men. Thomas Harvey, who interviewed Penn in the late 17th century, later wrote, “Josiah Coal went with him to London, also to his father's house, to see how he was likely to be entertained. His father kept his temper while J. C. was there, but before going to bed, observing him use thee or thou, he was very angry. [His father declared] he might thee or thou who he pleased, except the King, the Duke of York, and himself; these he should not thee or thou." Writing of this incident, biographer Maria Webb insisted, “But still William would not give his father to expect that he could in conscience make any such exceptions. On parting from him for the night, the admiral, with evidence of much displeasure, told his son to be ready to go out with him in the coach next morning when called on. William could sleep none that night, his mind being disturbed...."

The next day, according to the record Penn gave Harvey, his father rode with him to a park where they could speak privately. Harvey continued, “[Penn Sr.] commenced by asking him what he could think of himself, after being trained up in learning and courtly accomplishments, nothing being spared to fit him to take the position of an ambassador at foreign courts, or that of a minister at home, that he should now become a Quaker. William told him that it was in obedience to the manifestation of God's will in his conscience, but that it was a cross to his own nature. He also reminded him of that former meeting in Cork, and told him that he believed he was himself at that time convinced of the truth of the doctrine of the Quakers; only that the grandeur of the world had been felt to be a too great sacrifice to give up.”

Penn thought the argument was over when his father ordered the coach to take them to a nearby tavern for a drink. However, after entering a private room and ordering a glass of wine for himself, the Admiral suddenly strode to the door and locked it. Webb explained, “Father and son were now face to face, under the influence of stern displeasure on the one hand, and on the other, prayerful feeling to God for strength rightly to withstand or bear what was coming. William, remembering his early experience on returning from Oxford, expected something desperate. The thought arose that the admiral was going to cane him. But, instead of that, the father, looking earnestly at him, und laying his hands down on the table, solemnly told him he was going to kneel down to pray to Almighty God that his son might not be a Quaker, and that he might never again go to a Quaker meeting. William, opening the casement, declared that before he would listen to his father putting up such a prayer to God, he would leap out of the window."

Fortunately, a family friend happened to be passing the tavern and, upon seeing the Penn coach parked out front, decided to stop in and see them. He arrived just in time to potentially prevent a tragedy. According to Harvey, the friend "turned to the father, and told him he might think himself happy in having a son who could despise the grandeur of the world, and refrain from the vices which so many were running into."

Though other members of Admiral Penn's circle made similar observations about the positive change in young Penn, father and son remained at an impasse, and Penn's father, fearful for his own future in the court, began to consider the possibility of disinheriting him. However, this thought proved to be too much for him, and he instead continued hope that his son would lose interest in his newfound faith.

Like many new converts, Penn was passionate about his beliefs and soon sought to convert his friends. In a letter dated July 10, 1668, Penn wrote, "It was a True Word spoke by Jesus Christ, to undeceive all those Careless Wanton Jews, among whom he manifested his Glorious Truth, through That Body prepared of God for that very End, That the Way which leads to Everlasting Life and Rest, was very Strait and Narrow. My Friend, How much it may import the Welfare of thy Immortal Soul, to reflect upon that Course of Life, and Way thou now art walking in, before an Evident Stroke from Heaven call thee hence, and send thy so much indulged Flesh and Blood into the Grave; an Entertainment for no better than Noisome Worms. I beg thee, as ever thou wouldst be saved from that unspeakable Anguish, which is reserved for Worldlings, and from whence there is no Redemption, to keep thy self from those Vanities, Follies, and Pollutions, which unavoidably bring that Miserable State."

Around this time, Penn met the famous preacher George Fox, considered by most to be the founder of the Quaker denomination. Fox was a firebrand, passionate in his belief that "God who made the world did not dwell in temples made with hands." The problem was that Fox elaborated on this belief by insisting, "This at first seemed a strange word, because both priests and people used to call their temples, or churches, dreadful places, holy ground, and the temples of God. But the Lord showed me clearly that He did not dwell in these temples which men had commanded and set up, but in people's hearts; for both Stephen and the apostle Paul bore testimony that He did not dwell in temples made with hands, not even in that which He had once commanded to be built, since He put an end to it; but that His people were His temple, and He dwelt in them."

This was a direct rebuke against all established churches, including the Church of England, of which the king was head. As a result, as Penn came to embrace these ideas, he became more and more distant from his parents, their lives, and their values. Penn wrote in his introduction to the *Journal of George Fox*, "He was a man that God endowed with a clear and wonderful depth, a discerner of others' spirits, and very much a master of his own. And though the side of his understanding which lay next to the world, and especially the expression of it, might sound uncouth and unfashionable to nice ears, his matter was nevertheless very profound, and would not only bear to be often considered but the more it was so, the more weighty and instructing it appeared. And as abruptly and brokenly as sometimes his sentences would fall from him about divine things, it is well known they were often as texts to many fairer declarations. And indeed it shewed beyond all contradiction that God sent him, that no arts or parts had any share in the matter or manner of his ministry, and that so many great, excellent, and necessary truths as he came forth to preach to mankind, had therefore nothing of man's wit or wisdom to recommend them. So that as to man he was an original, being no man's copy. And his ministry and writings shew they are from one that was not taught of man, nor had learned what he said by study. Nor were they notional or speculative, but sensible and practical truths, tending to conversion and regeneration, and the setting up the kingdom of God in the hearts of men, and the way of it was his work."

Caught up in Fox's charismatic appeal, Penn wrote his first religious pamphlet, *Truth Exalted: To Princes, Priests and People*. In it, he boldly insisted that the Quakers were the only true manifestation of Christianity and that all other churches were heretical. Apparently, it was not particularly well-written, at least according to Pepys, who wrote in his diary on October 12, 1668 that he went "after supper to read a ridiculous nonsensical book set out by Will. Pen, for the Quakers; but so full of nothing but nonsense, that I was ashamed to read in it."

This, his first shot over the bow of the churches, earned Penn his much coveted attention and landed him in the Tower of London. While there, he decided to further stoke the flames stirring up around him by penning "The Sandy Foundation Shaken." Basing his text on the Biblical parable of the house built on sand, he wrote a scathing critique of those who did not embrace Quaker teachings. The Bishop of London, upon hearing of this latest outrage, ordered Penn held in the Tower until he recanted his more heretical comments, specifically those in which he appeared to deny the nature of the Trinity as being God the Father, Jesus the Son, and the Holy Spirit.

From his unheated and solitary cell, Penn countered that he did not at all deny the Trinity and wrote *Innocency with her open face, presented by way of Apology for the book entitled the Sandy Foundation Shaken*, in which he proclaimed, "This conclusive argument for the proof of Christ, the Saviour's, being God, should certainly persuade all sober persons of my innocency, and my adversaries malice. He that is the everlasting Wisdom, divine Power, the true Light, the only Saviour, the creating Word of all things, whether visible or invisible, and their upholder, by his own power, is, without contradiction God – but all these qualifications, and divine properties, arc by the concurrent testimonies of Scripture, ascribed to the Lord Jesus Christ; therefore, without a scruple, I call and believe him, really to be, the mighty God."

Since he still had paper and ink left over from his task, Penn made good use of his incarceration to compose yet another pamphlet, this one bearing the raging title, *No Cross, No Crown: A Discourse Shewing The Nature and Discipline of the Holy Cross of Christ and that the Denial of Self, and Daily Hearing of Christ's Cross, is the Alone Way to Rest and Kingdom of God.* Asserting, as did many Protestants, that the Christian Church had become corrupted in the years following Christ's ascension into heaven, Penn encouraged his readers to turn their minds and hearts back to the simplicity of Christ's basic teachings and to the methods of worship he claimed were practiced by 1st century Christians. What it may have lacked in orthodoxy it more than made up for in scholarship, for Penn quoted more than 65 previous writers dating from Biblical times to his own era. What makes the work even more amazing was that he completed it without any access to the original documents, relying instead on the memories of what he had previously studied.

By this time, Penn's dedication was beginning to make an impact on the king, who, though he refused to meet with the young "heretic," nonetheless had to respect the man who wrote to the king that he "mayst tell my father, who I know will ask thee, these words: that my prison shall be my grave before I will budge a jot; for I owe my conscience to no mortal man; I have no need to fear, God will make amends for all; they are mistaken in me; I value not their threats and resolutions, for the shall know I can weary out their malice and peevishness, and in me shall they all behold a resolution above fear…" The monarch discreetly ordered one of his own chaplains to try to find an excuse to release Penn. The chaplain succeeded, and Penn was freed in July 1669, 8 months after his arrest.

Heading for America

By this time, Penn was 25 years old. Though he was consumed with theology, in September, he approached Issac Pennington, a fellow Quaker, and asked his permission to court his stepdaughter, Gulielma Maria Posthuma Springett. However, if the family hoped for a wedding in the coming year, they were to be disappointed. Anxious to mollify his father without compromising his principles, Penn returned to Ireland to continue his law career, and he made some powerful friends, including the Earl of Arran, who proved to be a staunch supporter of the Quakers and assisted Penn in getting them released from Irish prisons.

Unfortunately, things were not improving for the growing sect in England, where Parliament passed the Conventicle Act in 1670. "For providing further and more speedy Remedies against the growing and dangerous practices of Seditious Sectaries and other disloyall Persons who under pretence of tender Consciences have or may at their Meetings contrive Insurrections," the act made it a crime for anyone 16 years old or older to "be present at any Assembly Conventicle or Meeteing under colour or pretence of any Exercise of Religion in other manner then according to the Liturgy and practice of the Church of England." While technically the law applied to any non-approved group, it targeted Quakers and Anabaptists in particular. According to Thomas Ellwood, a religious writer of that day, "This act broke down and o'er ran the bounds and banks anciently set for the security of Englishmen's lives, liberties, and properties, namely, trials by jury; instead thereof, authorizing justices of the peace (and that too, privately, out of sessions) to convict, fine, and by their warrants distrain upon offenders against it, directly contrary to the Great Charter."

Upon his return to London in June 1670, Penn found his father willing to accept his new faith, though he would certainly never embrace it. The two men renewed their relationship, and all was well for a few weeks until August 14, when Penn was arrested along with Quaker leader William Mead. The indictment against them read that on August 14, 1670, they "so assembled and congregated together…in the open Street, did take upon himself to preach and speak, and then, and there, did preach and speak unto the aforesaid William Mead, and other Persons there…by reason whereof a great concourse and tumult of People in the Street aforesaid, then and there, along time did remain and continue, in contempt of the said Lord the King, and of his Law, to the great disturbance of his Peace, to the great terror and disturbance of many of his Liege people and Subjects, to the ill example of all others…."

In response to the above charges, Penn admitted to the charges but denied that what he did should be illegal, saying, "We confess ourselves to be so far from recanting, or declining to vindicate the assembling of ourselves, to Preach, Pray, or Worship the Eternal, Holy, Just God, that we declare to all the World, that we do believe it to be our indispensable duty, to meet incessantly upon so good an account; nor shall all the powers upon Earth, be able to divert us from reverencing and adoring our God, who made us. …I have broken no Law, nor am I guilty of the Indictment, that is laid to my charge, and to the end the Bench, the Jury, and myself, with these that hear us, may have a most direct understanding of this procedure, I desire you would let me know by what Law it is you prosecute me, and upon what Law you ground my indictment."

Their trial, held two weeks later, was a watershed for English jurisprudence. When the jury voted to acquit the men, the judge hearing the case, Thomas Howell, ordered them kept without food until they returned a guilty verdict. Learning of this, Penn spoke out vehemently: "The agreement of twelve men is a verdict in law, and such a one being given by the jury, I require the clerk of the peace to record it, as he will answer it at his peril. And if the jury bring in another verdict contrary to this, I affirm they are perjured men in law. (And looking upon the jury, said,) you are Englishmen, mind your privileges, give not away your right." The jury remained strong and sued the judge for false imprisonment, winning their case and establishing the precedent that a jury's decision is indeed final.

Sadly, by the time the trial was over, Penn had a new, more personal sorrow to face - his father, with whom he had shared such a tumultuous relationship, was dying. Anxious for his son's future, Admiral Penn wrote to the Duke of York, then the heir apparent to the English throne, and solicited from him a promise that young Penn would enjoy the protection of the Crown for life. The Duke not only agreed to this request but, in recognition of the elder Penn's service to the crown, agreed to make William Penn a royal counselor. Thus, when his father died on September 16, 1670, Penn found himself not only a wealthy man, but also a rather powerful one.

In spite of his security, Penn still could not entirely avoid imprisonment, and perhaps did not even want to, for many of his letters during this time indicate that he was practicing an early form of civil disobedience with his public meetings. On February 5, 1671, he was arrested for refusing to take an oath to the king, a practice forbidden in Quaker teaching. This time the court did not even try him but instead simply kept him imprisoned until August.

In the years following his father's death, Penn devoted much of his time to preaching in Germany on behalf of the Quaker faith, creating a German Settlement that appealed not just to Quakers but to other Anabaptist sects, including the Amish and Mennonites. Fittingly, these groups would one day become part of the backbone of Penn's New World colony.

Once out of jail, he again met with Fox, who was about to leave on an extended trip to America. Fox's reports would later prove a catalyst to Penn's colonization plans, but Penn also had personal business to attend to at this time, finally marrying the long-suffering Miss Springett on April 4, 1672. Their marriage proved a happy one and produced seven children, though only three, Springett, Letitia, and William, Jr., survived to adulthood.

Now a man with familial responsibilities, Penn cut back on the amount he traveled and devoted most of his time to writing. According to biographer Joseph Barker, "Meetings were held at one place or another almost every day in the week, many of which he attended and addressed. The disputes too in the religious world which prevailed in these times, and in which the Quakers were particularly engaged, called him frequently forth as an author…In the preceding year Charles the Second had issued a declaration of indulgence to tender consciences in matters of religion, in consequence of which not less than five hundred Quakers had been released from prison. This indulgence was extended also to dissenters at large. Now one would have thought that the leaders of the different religious sects, all of which had felt the iron hand of persecution, would have employed this respite in solacing each other, and in promoting love among each other. But they did the contrary. They began to persecute each other, and their conduct towards the Quakers was most disgraceful."

Apparently, the cause of the conflict was that which had plagued many denominations for centuries: membership and the tithes that went with it. Barker concluded that "many, especially of the Baptists, began to be attached to them, and left their own particular societies and joined them. The leaders of several of the religious sects, finding their congregations growing less by such defections, seemed to think they could not use their liberty better than by trying to crush the Quakers. Hence many publications appeared against them of a most abusive character. These things gave Penn so much work, that he had but very little time left for repose during the whole of the present year."

There was also some dissent within the ranks of the Quakers themselves, for some members preferred Penn's more esoteric, intellectual interpretations of Scripture while others were more attracted to Fox and his down-to-earth approach to the faith. Since the men themselves were close friends and were unwilling to allow their personal egos to get in the way of the good of the churches, they were able to work together to heal these rifts before the problems grew. In 1672, Penn and his wife traveled with evangelist George Whitehead to Bristol, where they welcomed Fox home and help a number of public revival services and debates, some of which drew thousands in attendance.

The following year saw King Charles II try to stem some of the tide of religious persecution sweeping the country by passing the Law of Indulgence, which nixed previous laws passed against religious sects. However, Parliament wasted no time in passing new laws against free worship, leading Penn to write, "England's Present Interest Considered." Writing in 1882, Samuel Janney observed of this work:

> "Penn offers many weighty considerations of a political nature to show the necessity of toleration. In this work Penn traces the history and progress of civil liberty in England from the earliest times, showing that it existed long before the Reformation, and had no necessary connection with the established church. Those rights and privileges which he terms English, and which are the birthrights of Englishmen may be reduced to three:
>
> 1. An ownership, and undisturbed possession of property.
>
> 2. A voting of every law that is made, whereby that ownership may be maintained.
>
> 3. An influence upon, and real share in that judiciary power that must apply every such law, which is the ancient, necessary and laudable use of juries."

Janney further quoted Penn as writing, "The first of these rights relates to security of estate and liberty of person from the violence of arbitrary power…to maintain the good, approved, and ancient laws of this kingdom, and to inhibit all spoil and unjust judgement."

Janney continued, "The second of these privileges he proves to be of ancient date, for the

Britons had their 'council,' the Saxons their 'wittangemote' or parliament, and William the Conqueror in his laws refers to the 'Common Council of the whole kingdom' as acting with him. The third privilege was well established among the Saxons; for in the laws of King Ethelred, three hundred years before the entrance of the Norman Duke, it is said, 'In every hundred let there be a court, and let twelve ancient freemen, together with the lord of the hundred, be sworn that they will not condemn the innocent nor acquit the guilty.' This privilege was also acknowledged under the Norman kings…Hence he concludes that the Great Charter, made in the ninth of Henry III., was not the nativity but restoration of ancient privileges from abuses. No grant of new rights, but a new grant, or confirmation rather, of ancient laws and liberties, violated by King John and restored by his successor at the expense of a long and bloody war, which showed them as resolute to keep as their ancestors had been careful to make those excellent laws."

Though he continued to fight for religious tolerance in England, Penn was also looking into alternative options for those wanting to practice their faith unmolested. By this time, the Plymouth experiment in Massachusetts was bearing good fruit and proving that America could indeed be colonized. At the same time, however, the Puritans who founded the colony had made it very clear that non-Puritans were not welcome within their province, so emigrating there was not an option.

At the same time, Edward Byllynge, a Quaker leader, knew that other land was available, particularly a parcel called West Jersey. Penn became involved with the 1675 purchase when he was called upon to mediate a dispute between Byllynge and his agent, John Fenwick.

With the matter resolved, Fenwick led a group of families to America, where they founded Salem, New Jersey, while Penn remained in London as a trustee for the colony. In that capacity, he composed *The Charter or Fundamental Laws, of West New Jersey,* which contained this startling clause: "That no men, nor number of men upon earth, hath power or authority to rule over men's consciences in religious matters, therefore it is consented, agreed and ordained, that no person or persons whatsoever within the said Province, at any time or times hereafter, shall be any ways upon any presence whatsoever, called in question, or in the least punished or hurt, either in person, estate, or priviledge, for the sake of his opinion, judgment, faith or worship towards God in matters of religion. But that all and every such person, and persons may from time to time, and at all times, freely and fully have, and enjoy his and their judgments, and the exercises of their consciences in matters of religious worship throughout all the said Province."

In the months that followed, more and more Quaker families sailed to New Jersey, thanks in part to the fact that the persecution spread and intensified in England. Both Fox and Penn were imprisoned on several occasions during the mid-1670s, and drawing on the promises made to his father, Penn repeatedly appealed to the Duke of York who in turn spoke out against this religious persecution. When the men were finally released, they traveled together to Germany and

Holland, where, along with a number of other Quaker leaders, they were well-received. Even the Princess Elizabeth Palatine granted them an audience.

Upon returning to England, Penn began to push the Duke to support his move, with as many Quakers as would join him, to head America. Knowing that his father had loaned large sums of money to Charles II, in May 1680, Penn petitioned the crown for the money he was owed, reminding the king, "That having sought payment for debts due to his father in Ireland by the oppression of the Lord Treasurr, this account was not settled at his father's decease…he was forced to borrow every penny of it, by reason that since the year 1672, His Majesty's Treasury of England was under the Stop of the Exchequer, so that the debt now amounts to £16,000…and 9 years having passed, the petitioner humbly prays for the relief of his own and his mother's great debts and otherwise certain ruin."

In lieu of the money he was owed, Penn wisely asked for something much less valuable to the king but of much greater value to him, namely "a tract of land in America, lying north of Maryland, on the east bounded with Delaware River, on the west, limited as Maryland is, and northward to extend as far as plantable, which is altogether Indian." In return, he promised to "undertake to render it a profitable plantation to the crown. And the petitioner further promises to raise that speedy and sufficient sum of money from this grant: to satisfy his encumbrances, that he may settle his accounts and extinguish his debt of at least £11,000 and be of such service to His Majesty in this place and time as shall be most beneficial to the Kingdom."

Penn eventually won the day, though it took a while. On March 4, 1681, the king granted a charter for a new colony to "William Penn, esquire, son and heir of Sir William Penn, deceased (out of a commendable desire to enlarge our English empire, and promote such useful commodities as may be of benefit to us and our dominions, as also to reduce the savage natives, by gentle and just manners, to the love of civil society and Christian religion)…." The land in question consisted of "all that tract or part of land in America, with the islands therein contained, as the same is bounded on the east by Delaware River, from twelve miles distance northward of New Castle Town, unto the three and fortieth degree of northern latitude…. The said land to extend westward five degrees in longitude, to be computed from the said eastern bounds, and the said lands to be bounded on the north by the beginning of the three and fortieth degree of northern latitude, and on the south by a circle drawn at twelve miles distance from New Castle, northward and westward unto the beginning of the fortieth degree of northern latitude, and then by a straight line westward to the limits of longitude above mentioned."

In the end, so anxious was Charles II to get his debts settled and the Quakers out of England that he gave Penn a total of 43,000 square miles of land, immediately making him the largest non-royal landowner in the world. The king added one small but charming caveat, which Penn wrote about on January 5, 1681: "This day, after many waitings, watchings, solicitings, and disputes in councils my country was confirmed to me under the great seal of England, with large powers and privileges, by the name of Pennsylvania, a name the king would give it in honour of my father. …I proposed Sylvania, and they added Penn to it, though I much opposed it, and went to the king to have it struck out. He said it was past and would take it upon him; nor could twenty guineas move the under-secretary to vary the name (bribes were then common), for I feared it should be looked on as a vanity in me and not as a respect in the king to my father, as it really was."

This small aggravation could not dampen Penn's spirits too much. He concluded, "Thou may'st communicate my grant to friends, and expect shortly my proposals. 'Tis a dear and just thing; and my God, who has given it me through many difficulties, will, I believe, bless and make it the seed of a nation. I shall take a tender care to the government that it be well laid first."

A painting depicting Penn and King Charles II

Penn's mind raced with the potential bursting out of the opportunity presented to him, and, wasting no time, he pounced on the deal. It now became his ambition to start a colony like no other from scratch, fill it with Quakers and religious refugees, and create a utopia of brotherhood and harmony. This became the ultimate goal – one he fondly dubbed "The Holy Experiment." William proposed the name of "Sylvania," or Latin for "woods," for his new territory. This idea was rejected by the king, who argued for it to be named after the fallen admiral instead. And thus, "Pennsylvania" would be born.

Anxious to learn what exactly he had gained before taking families into the wilderness, Penn sent his cousin, William Markham, to America, authorizing him to look the area over and make such decisions as he deemed necessary for the new province. He also ordered Markham to begin work on a home for him and his family to live in when they arrived. In the meantime, he stayed home and wrote "Some Account of the Province of Pennsylvania in America" to recruit settlers for his new enterprise, offering to sell the land at a rate of five acres per pound.

As he went about setting up a government for the new colony, Penn, as had so many before him, sought to create a heaven on earth. To this end he not only guaranteed his settlers freedom of worship but also that those accused of a crime would be tried by an impartial jury and that, should they be convicted, the goal of their imprisonment would not be punishment but rehabilitation. As he put it, "all our prisons will be workhouses." One of Penn's contemporaries, Chancellor Kent of England, observed, "The Pennsylvanian lawyer cannot but be struck on the perusal of this work— equally remarkable for profound knowledge, and condensed thought — with the analogy between his proposed improvements, and of all essential reforms jn the English laws, suggested by the greatest reformers of the law in England, and the long familiar practice of Pennsylvania."

In spite of the fact that they were being harassed more and more, most Quakers were not yet ready to leave their homes and extended families and move to a land they had never seen. After all, they reasoned, being arrested and potentially held in jail was not as bad as dying of hunger or Indian attacks in the American forests. Penn, believing to the core of his being that he was doing God's will, made it his mission in life to convince the people he had sacrificed so much for to move to Pennsylvania. To this end, he began writing a new kind of pamphlet, one that not only encouraged his readers to seek heaven some day but to find the courage to move to what he made seem like a heaven on earth. As historian Jean Souderland noted, "Like real estate developers today, WP was eager to advertise the advantages of moving to his new property. He wrote eight promotional tracts 'to give some public notice' of Pennsylvania 'to the world.' If he were trying to sell land today, he would have produced a flashy brochure filled with many pictures, but WP's promotional tracts were very different--sober and restrained in tone. He had no real need to exaggerate or oversell, for the printed word had enormous impact upon seventeenth-century readers…Since he was already widely known as a Quaker leader, he made no mention of his religion or of his plans for a holy experiment in this pamphlet. Clearly WP was hoping to appeal to a wider, non-Quaker audience, but he also sent the tract to Friends throughout England, Ireland, Scotland, and Wales, and it was quickly translated into Dutch and German. Since WP had not yet been to Pennsylvania…his description of his new land was necessarily brief, and his tips for packing and preparing for the journey rather vague. He concentrated instead on a lively defense of colonization, and stressed the advantages of leaving the Old World for the New, where land, material profits, improved family life, and good government awaited the industrious adventurer. The contrast he painted between the decadence of the Old World and the hard-working innocence of the New World would become a regular fixture in American literature."

Penn's writing skills once more proved effective. By the end of the year he had more than 250 settlers ready to settle 300,000 of his new plantation. While most of the settlers were men like himself, Quakers, and married with families and enough money put aside to buy the land, others came from among Europe's many abused religious groups, including the Amish and Jews. These first settlers had to have been impressed with the unprecedented freedom that Penn offered, including the use of waterways for fishing and travel: "all rivers, rivulets, woods and underwoods, waters, watercourses, quarries, mines, and minerals (except mines royal) shall be freely and fully enjoyed and wholly by the purchasers into whose lot they fall." The "mines royal" consisted of gold and other precious metals that he had promised to the king, but these would not amount to much.

The most astounding law made, however, was not for the protection of the invaders but of the invaded. Penn declared, "That no man shall, by any ways or means in word or deed, affront or wrong any Indian, but he shall incur the same penalty of the law as if he had committed it against his fellow planter. And if any Indian shall abuse in word or deed any planter of this province, that he shall not be his own judge upon the Indian, but he shall make his complaint to the governor of the province, or his lieutenant or deputy, or some inferior magistrate near him, who shall to the utmost of his power take care with the king of the said Indian, that all reasonable satisfaction be made to the said injured planter…That all differences between the planters and the natives shall also be ended by twelve men, that is, by six planters and six natives; that so we may live friendly together and, as much as in us lies, prevent all occasions of heart burnings and mischiefs. That the Indians shall have liberty to do all things relating to the improvement of their ground and providing sustenance for their families, that any of the planters shall enjoy."

It was these and other similar principles that informed Penn's development of "The FRAME of the GOVERNMENT of the Province of Pennsylvania in AMERICA: Together with certain LAWS Agreed upon in England by the GOVERNOR and Divers FREEMEN of the aforesaid PROVINCE."

Like some many of his other efforts, it was unique in that place and time. Author Marcus Jernegan explained, "In the Frame of 1682 and in other documents he bound himself not to interfere with the liberties of his colonists. Yet he did not intend by these renunciations to give sanction to all that might be done in the name of freedom or to refuse those safeguards for the rights of property and wealth which were essential items in his philosophy. "Licentiousness" included a number of things which a perfect libertarian could not prohibit or even frown upon. A convinced democrat could hardly have written, as did Penn: "And yet the latitudinarian that I love is one that is only so in charity, for the freedom I recommend is no skepticism in judgment and much less so in practice."

Indeed, Penn prohibited a number of practices in Pennsylvania that were perfectly acceptable in other colonies, including lying, swearing, gambling, cock-fighting, bear-baiting and drunkenness. He would not allow such typically acceptable entertainments as plays and dances, either. At the same time, Penn embraced the death penalty for those found guilty of murder or treason. In this way he was a man of his times, for even a pacifist could not sanction allowing someone to live who had taken a human life or threatened the safety of the rest of society with political uprising.

In forming an outline for the government of Pennsylvania, Penn relied heavily on the work of John Locke, a proponent of the principal of individual rights. He also did something that had never been done before by adding amendments to the original document, opening the door for future revisions in his work. In that way, he trusted future generations, conceding that "when all is said, there is hardly one frame of government in the world so ill designed by its first founders that, in good hands, would not do well enough; and story tells us, the best, in ill ones, can do nothing that is great or good.... Governments, like clocks, go from the motion men give them, and as governments are made and moved by men, so by them they are ruined too. Wherefore governments rather depend upon men than men upon governments. Let men be good, and the government cannot be bad; if it be ill, they will cure it. But, if men be bad, let the government be ever so good, they will endeavor to warp and spoil it to their turn."

John Locke

Another, more artistic part of Penn's plan for his utopia included a large capital city, one that would be the first planned community in America. He instructed his men, "Such a place being found out for navigation, healthy situation, and good soil for provision lay out ten thousand acres contiguous to it in the best manner you can as the bounds and extent of the liberties of the said town. The proportion in the said town is to be thus: every share or five thousand acres shall have a hundred acres of land out of that ten thousand acres. If more than one be concerned in the share, as it may easily fall out, then they [are] to agree of the dividing the same as they shall think fit, still keeping to proportion as if £100 will have a hundred acres, £5 will have five acres."

He later added, "Be sure to settle the figure of the town so as that the streets hereafter may be uniform down to the water from the country bounds. Let the place for the storehouse be on the middle of the quay, which will yet serve for market and state houses, too. This may be ordered when I come; only let the houses built be in a line, or upon a line as much as may be…The distance of each house from the creek or harbor should be, in my judgment, a measured quarter of a mile, at least two hundred paces, because of building hereafter streets downwards to the harbor. Let every house be placed, if the person pleases, in the middle of its plot as to the breadth way of it, that so there may be ground on each side for gardens or orchards or fields, that it may be a green country town, which will never be burnt and always be wholesome."

Pennsylvania

A depiction of Slate Roof House, one of Penn's residences in Philadelphia

With his plans now firmly in place, Penn left England on August 30, 1682, bound for Pennsylvania on the prosaically named *Welcome of Pennsylvania.* Tragedy struck along the way when smallpox broke out, claiming the lives of nearly a third of the passengers. When the ship landed after nearly two months at sea, 68 weary, frightened passengers stumbled to shore, following Governor Penn to their new lives.

Now that he was there, the promise of Pennsylvania was truly unveiled; the enterprising William envisioned an enormous city stretching along the Delaware River. One of his companions, Thomas Holmes, was appointed the head city planner. Week after week, Holmes trudged through the thick of the woods, mapping out future roads and establishments. Unlike the congested and complicated streets back home, the new city would be constructed in a clean, grid-like pattern, free of walls and dark alleys, which were said to be the breeding grounds of evil.

To achieve this, more territory was required. This would be a challenge on its own, as neighboring villages were already packed with Native American and other European settlers who had been there long before them. William knew that kindness would be the only key to winning the trust of the tentative villagers. He engaged in fair and peaceful negotiations with European settlers, and convinced them to sell their land to him. Soon, Europe was abuzz with rumors of this elysian community, and many more hopped on a boat to join them. From then on, the growing city was known as "Philadelphia."

William's attitude towards the Native Americans was yet another factor that set him apart from other American settlers. In late 1682, William and his companions approached and slowly befriended the Lenape Tribe, who lived by the great river. To demonstrate his commitment to an equal partnership, William devoted his time to learning their language and customs, and he attended their ceremonies with no judgment. In time, the Lenape and the American Quakers arrived at an agreement.

Of course, Penn's intentions were not completely altruistic, for while he intended to pay the natives for their land, he also wanted to get a good price. With that in mind, he instructed his commissioners in America, "Be tender of offending the Indians, and hearken by honest spies. If you can hear that anybody inveighs the Indians not to sell, or to stand off and raise the value upon you. You cannot want those that will inform you. But to soften them to me and the people, let them know that you are come to sit down lovingly among them. Let my letter and conditions with my purchasers about just dealing with them be read in their tongue, that they may see we have their good in our eye, equal with our own interest. And after reading my letter and the said conditions, then present their kings with what I send them, and make a friendship and league with them according to those conditions, which carefully observe, and get them to comply with you. Be grave; they love not to be smiled on."

The Lenape handed over their land in exchange for a solid price, and their terms were detailed in what is now known as "Penn's Treaty," a document that seemingly symbolized a new era of peace and prosperity between the natives and American settlers. Little did the Lenape know that the written document held nothing but empty words.

With his own home not yet ready, Penn moved in with Thomas Fairman just outside the city. Upon seeing the site of his new city with his own eyes, he made a few small changes to his original plans, calling for the trees that ran east and west to be named for native trees while those running north and south were numbered.

The first Pennsylvania Assembly met in the spring of 1683 and reviewed Penn's "Frame." They made a few small revisions, most significantly reducing Penn's vote as governor from three to one, before they adopted the document as the "New Charter." For his own part, Penn not only accepted their decision but announced that he would not be levying taxes on items imported and exported in the state, sacrificing income that would, as governor, fall to him.

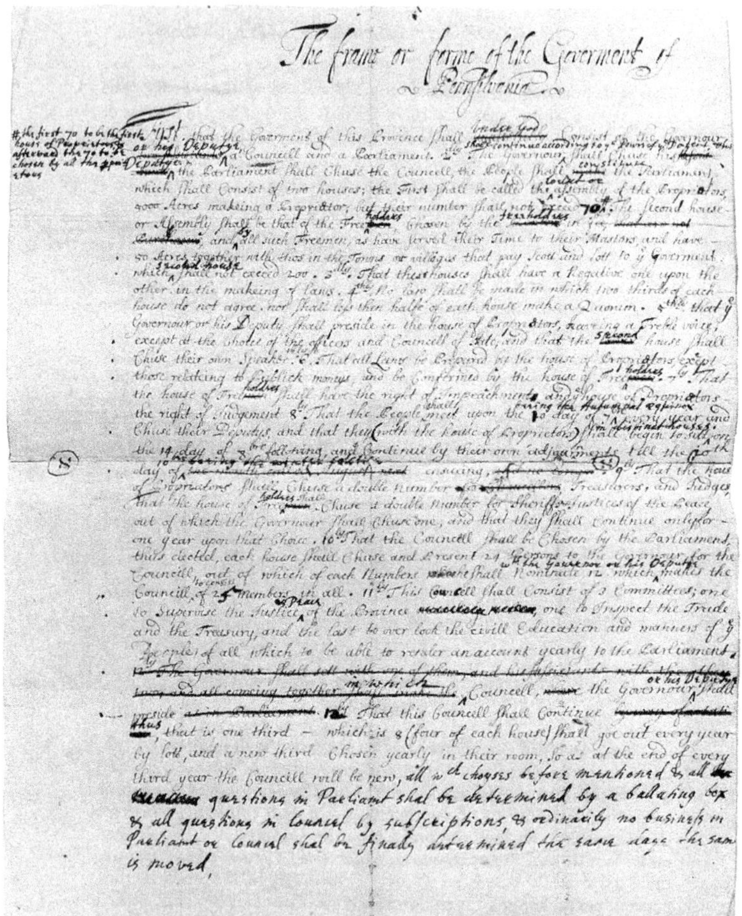
The frame or forme of the Goverment of Pensilvania

A picture of the first draft of the Frame of Government

In April, Penn moved into his new home at Pennsbury, in Bucks County. There he met with representatives of the Lenni Lenape people and spent two days walking around the area and periodically smoking a pipe with the natives, solidifying the sale of what would become known as the first part of the Walking Purchase. This extended his holdings about 30 miles north to what is now the Bucks/Northampton county border. Altogether, Penn traveled 120 miles into land still held by the native peoples, talking to them frequently and thus learning how to speak their language, which he described as "lofty, yet narrow; but, like the Hebrew in signification, full. Like short-hand in writing, one word serveth in the place of three, and the rest are supplied by the understanding of the hearer, imperfect in their tenses, wanting in their moods, participles, adverbs, conjunctions, interjections."

Penn later described the land he saw, writing, "The country itself, its soil, air water, seasons, and produce, both natural and artificial, are not to be despised. The land containeth divers sorts of earth, as sand, yellow and black, poor and rich; also gravel, both loamy and dusty; and in some places a fast, fat earth, like that of our best vales in England, especially by inland brooks and rivers: God in his wisdom having ordered it so, that the advantages of the country are divided; the back lands being generally three to one richer than those that lie by navigable rivers. We have much of another soil, and that is a black hazel mould upon a stony or rocky bottom…The air is sweet and clear, and the heavens serene, like the south parts of France, rarely overcast; and as the woods come by numbers of people to be more cleared, that itself will refine. The waters are generally good; for the rivers and brooks have mostly gravel and stony bottoms, and in numbers hardly credible." That fall, on October 8, 1683, 34 more Quakers arrived, this time from Germany, and settled in an area they named "Germantown."

Not everything was smooth sailing, however. Penn's carefully crafted alliance with Tamanend, the Lenape chief who had signed the treaty with him at Shackamaxon, soon soured. The alarmed Tamanend watched as throngs of construction workers invaded the land, swishing their axes and chopping down trees that once stood in the vibrant Lenape forests, to make room for the new city. The chief of the Turtle Clan had been under the impression that Penn and his men would preserve the land, and he quickly became convinced that these white men were looking to pull one over on him. Hearsay suggested that a dark, ulterior motive lay behind his sudden camaraderie with the natives – he was planning to herd up the natives and evict them from their own land, as he feared the unfamiliar faces would scare off the myriads of incoming British settlers. Eventually, the Lenape announced that they no longer wanted anything to do with Penn. The lamentable tidings deeply wounded the Quaker, who was said to have liked the natives. Most white men of his time vilified the natives as "savages," but Penn often spoke and wrote highly about the natives. He once said about them, "But in liberality they excel; nothing is too good for their friend. Give them a fine gun, coat, or other thing, it may pass 20 hands before it sticks...[They are] the most merry creatures that live, feast, and dance perpetually; they never have much, nor want much."

The hurdle with the natives was only one of the dozens sprouting up in William's path. In 1684, just 2 years after William's arrival, he would face Lord Baltimore of Maryland head on in a long-lasting territorial dispute. Trouble surfaced when Lord Baltimore came out of the woodwork to claim that he owned several portions of Pennsylvania, and he commanded the Philadelphian settlers to take a hike. William had no choice but to make the 3,000 mile journey back home, where he would work to garner proof for his rightful ownership to the land. At this point, William's old friend, the Duke of York, had risen to the throne as King James II, and he was a monarch both admired and notorious for his support of religious toleration. While there, Penn soon learned that, because of his own lack of attention to detail, he did not clearly understand where the 40 degrees latitude line actually lay. In the end, it took 80 years of legal wrangling to establish the respective borders between Pennsylvania and Maryland, which still exist today.

King James II of England

Lord Baltimore

Penn found other trouble waiting in England, too, learning that the more than one large prison was filled with Quakers being held for practicing their religion. So much had the tide turned against his people that there were even rumors that Parliament might revoke his charter. In the midst of this, King James II ruled in Penn's favor concerning the dispute with Lord Baltimore, though the conflict would continue to flare up from time to time. The king also pardoned and released all the religious prisoners being held in the nation.

Determined to see all his subjects free to follow their consciences, the king issued the Declaration of Indulgence, in which he proclaimed that "we do freely give them leave to meet and serve God after their own way and manner, be it in private houses or in places purposely hired or built for that use, so that they take especial care, that nothing be preached or taught amongst them which may any ways tend to alienate the hearts of our people from us or our government; and that their meetings and assemblies be peaceably, openly, and publicly held, and all persons freely admitted to them; and that they do signify and make known to some one or more of the next justices of the peace what place or places they set apart for those uses. And that all our subjects may enjoy such their religious assemblies with greater assurance and protection, we have thought it requisite, and do hereby command, that no disturbance of any kind be made or given unto them, under pain of our displeasure, and to be further proceeded against with the uttermost severity."

This was one of the earliest broad declarations of religious freedom in European history. However, King James II was a Catholic king with a Protestant parliament, and he had trouble enforcing the declaration. For his part, Penn traveled throughout England speaking out on behalf of the king and the declaration and encouraging his fellow Quakers to speak out in support of the king as well. In June 1688 he gave an impassioned plea before the London Yearly Meeting of the Society of Friends, urging them to create a committee to train members of the sect on the ins and outs of English government in the hopes that some of them would be willing to serve in political offices under the crown. Such an idea was outside the norms of traditional Quaker teaching at this time, and many, including Fox, opposed it.

As it turned out, Fox's followers proved wise in not putting too much faith in the king, for just a few months later, in November 1688, Parliament called on William of Orange to rule with his wife, Queen Mary, as Protestant monarchs in England. The new sovereigns arrested Penn, along with a number of King James II's other supporters, but they had no desire to see him severely punished and soon set him free. The following year, in 1689, Parliament passed its own religious liberties law, the Act of Toleration, which guaranteed most of the freedoms King James II's declaration had assured.

An engraving depicting William and Mary

Final Years

This was a time of both joy and sorrow for Penn, for while he was thrilled to see his friends released and the Crown make moves to expand their rights, he was also facing increased financial troubles. He was losing money on his investments in Pennsylvania, to the tune of about 3,000 pounds a year, forcing him to move his family to smaller lodgings in Holland House in

Kensington.

Moreover, in spite of the dangers inherent in his actions, Penn remained loyal to the ousted king and was arrested on more than one occasion for corresponding with him. He also lost his old friend, Fox, in January 1691. Though he was still under suspicion from the Crown, he traveled to London to give a eulogy at Fox's funeral. William and Mary were not happy to hear this and suspected that he had political motives that might undermine their reign, so they had him arrested for treason. In 1692, William removed Pennsylvania from Penn's control and turned it over to the Governor of New York.

Such losses would have made a saintly man bitter, and they did indeed take their toll on Penn. His "Essay towards the Present and Future Peace of Europe" led to accusations of treason in Ireland, allowing the king and queen to confiscate his lands there. In response, he wrote "Some Fruits of Solitude" in which he mused, "For Disappointments, that come not by our own Folly, they are the Tryals or Corrections of Heaven: And it is our own Fault, if they prove not our Advantage. To repine at them does not mend the Matter: It is only to grumble at our Creator. But to see the Hand of God in them, with an humble submission to his Will, is the Way to turn our Water into Wine, and engage the greatest Love and Mercy on our side. We must needs disorder ourselves, if we only look at our Losses. But if we consider how little we deserve what is left, our Passion will cool, and our Murmurs will turn into Thankfulness."

Penn's optimism paid off on November 30, 1693, when the charges against him were finally dropped. As fate would have it, his relief was short-lived, for his wife was dying. On February 23, 1694, he found himself widowed. Seeking solace in writing, he composed "A Brief Account of The Rise and Progress of the People Called Quakers."

In August of that year, he regained control of his beloved Pennsylvania and found renewed happiness in shaping its future. His happiness increased on March 5, 1696, the date he married young Hannah Callowhill. She bore him eight children in 12 years, six of whom survived their father.

In 1697, Penn met with Russian tsar Peter the Great, then touring England. The young ruler was sufficiently impressed enough by Penn that he attended a Quaker meeting in Deptford.

The following year, Penn returned to Ireland to take possession of those estates that the Crown had returned to his possession. His greatest thrill, however, came when he was able to return, with his growing family, to Pennsylvania at the end of 1699. He would spend the next year of his life at Pennsbury, visiting both friends and past foes, such as Lord Baltimore.

Not all had gone according to plan while he was away. In his absence, the residents of Philadelphia, like mutinous children freed from the supervision of their parents, wreaked havoc. Unruly Philadelphians loitered in caves by the river and crowded in makeshift alleyways that cut through the city. The clean grid layout Penn so pined for was no more, and even worse, these alleys and cave parties multiplied with round-the-clock gambling, nonstop drinking, and promiscuous sexual activities. It appeared as if the majority of these displaced dissenters with evidently questionable morals had not an inkling of interest in Quakerism or wholesome community living.

When the 55-year-old Penn returned to Pennsylvania after a 15-year absence, he was confounded by the shocking state of affairs. It was a true fall from grace – Philadelphia's crime and incarceration rates were the highest of all the colonial cities. Prostitutes stalked the streets as canoodling couples posted in every corner showed grossly public displays of affection. Sloppy drunkards drifted from one pub to another in broad daylight. Men, women, and children were shortly fused, and wild, impromptu brawls had become the norm.

Other American Quakers were dealing with the much more pressing problem of persecution. In Boston, Massachusetts, Quakerism was among the most grievous of crimes. Quaker ministers and authors, like Ann Austin and Mary Fisher, were only some of the many that would feel others' wrath. Far from Pennsylvania, Quakers were spurned as heretics by Bostonian authorities, locked up, and had their works thrown into bonfires. In time, they were released, disgraced, and deported, never allowed to return.

The severity of the punishments depended on the region. Some were luckier than most and were only imprisoned as a warning before they were banished. Others were scourged, scarred for life with branding irons, and suffered other cruel and unusual punishment. Christopher Holder, a Quaker based in New England, had his ears sheared off. More stories of flogging, property confiscation, and eternal banishment sprung forth in New Amsterdam, Rhode Island, and New York. Even the Dutch West India Company despised them, often belittling the "abominable religion."

There were still some silver linings, though. By the time of Penn's return, there were more than 18,000 people in the colony and 3,000 in Philadelphia, making it one of the largest cities in North America. The trees he had ordered planted had also grown, providing pleasant shade during the summer and shielding residents from bitter winds during the winter. Those visiting the city could find shops rivaling those in any medium sized town in England, and Penn's public schools, a source of great pride to him, were turning out some of the best educated youth in the New World. Already doctors and scientists were being attracted to the colony, where did not need to fear Puritanical interference. In 1701, he freed the three slaves who had been working for him and encouraged his fellow Quakers to do the same, but the sect had not yet developed its strict teachings on that subject and not everyone followed his exhortations.

Penn might have hoped to remain in Pennsylvania permanently, but government powers in England began to talk again of taking control of Pennsylvania, so he had to return there to fight those efforts. He was able to win a limited victory, with the Pennsylvania Assembly agreeing to a new "Charter of Priviledges." This document took more power from Penn by allowing the Assembly to propose laws, a right that had previously belonged exclusively to the Governor and his council. Part of the state also split away to become Delaware.

Even with these issues resolved, Penn's problems were far from over. Philip Ford, a fellow Quaker whom Penn used to manage his business affairs, realized that Penn rarely read documents he gave him to sign. With this knowledge, he began to embezzle increasingly larger sums of money. When he remained undiscovered, he became bolder and managed to sneak past Penn a document which gave him ownership of Penn's share of Pennsylvania. He then began to charge his former friend exorbitant he could not pay. After Ford died in 1702, his heirs went to court to try to force Penn to pay the "rents" he owed them. After years of wrangling, they finally managed to have Penn thrown in debtors prison for a time. When the case finally made it to court in 1708, the Lord Chancellor ruled in Penn's favor, asserting that "the equity of redemption still remained in William Penn and his heirs…and as to taking the government, that could not be…"

By 1709, Penn's life seemed to be back in order. He and Hannah were apparently happy together, in spite of his frequent travels. On July 14, 1709 he wrote to her from London, "It is not with a little trouble that the enjoyment of mine own dearest is thus deferred; for ten days ago and more I purposed to have been with her, but those that I fear never care whether I see thee or not detain me, and I cannot say that I have no interest therein. Scores of guineas have melted since I saw thee, there is no enduring it any longer, but I waive much till I see thee, but I see my course positively and clearly to which I hope for my dearest H's compliance. It will be fourth day next before I can get away and intend by the two days' coach."

The following year, the newly elected Pennsylvania Assembly passed a number laws that relieved the financial burdens he had acquired in starting the colony, allowing him and his growing family moved to a comfortable home in Berkshire. They were active in the Quaker meeting in Reading, and he lived relatively peacefully for more than a year until he suffered a debilitating stroke that paralyzed him and weakened his memory. For the rest of his life, many of his business affairs were managed by Hannah, who wrote in January 1715, "When I keep the thoughts of business from him, he is very sweet, comfortable, and easy, and is cheerfully resigned to the Lord's will, and yet takes delight in his children, his friends, and domestic comforts, as formerly. It is the public and his family who feel the loss, and myself the trouble of his (I may say) translation."

Within a few years, his condition had deteriorated. Hannah noted, "I have, for these last three or four years, continued on in this large, house and expense, only to keep him as comfortable as I can; for he had all along delighted in walking and taking the air here, and does still, when the weather allows; and, at other times, diverts himself from room to room; and the satisfaction he takes therein is the greatest pleasure I have in enjoying so large a house, which I have (with the necessary expenses and loads I bear) long found too much for me and our shrunk income."

Finally, on July 30, 1718, William Penn died at the age of 74 and was laid to rest in Jordans, beside his first wife, Gulielma.

FRIENDS' MEETING-HOUSE AT JORDANS, AND THE GRAVE OF WILLIAM PENN.

300 years later, William Penn is still remembered as more than just a vigorous visionary. Undoubtedly one of the colonial era's most important men, no less an authority than Thomas Jefferson once called him one of the greatest lawmakers to have ever lived.

Online Resources

Other books about colonial American history by Charles River Editors

Other books about William Penn on Amazon

Further Reading

Dunn, Mary Maples. William Penn: Politics and Conscience (1967)

Dunn, Richard S. and Mary Maples Dunn, eds. The World of William Penn (1986), essays by scholars

Endy, Jr., Melvin B. William Penn and Early Quakerism (1973)

Geiter, Mary K. "William Penn" (Longman,2000)

Moretta, John. William Penn and the Quaker Legacy (2006)

Morgan, Edmund S. "The World and William Penn," Proceedings of the American Philosophical Society (1983) 127#5 pp. 291–315 JSTOR 986499.

Nash, Gary B. Quakers and Politics: Pennsylvania, 1681–1726 (1968)

Peare, Catherine O. William Penn (1957), a standard biography

Soderlund, Jean R. "Penn, William" in American National Biography Online (2000)

Free Books by Charles River Editors

Discounted Books by Charles River Editors

We have titles at a discount price of just 99 cents everyday. To see which of our titles are currently 99 cents, click on this link.

Printed in Great Britain
by Amazon

70931301R00031